STOCKHOLM

SHOPPING GUIDE 2023

A FRIENDLY GUIDE TO THE BEST SHOPPING IN THE CITY

ANNA C. GUSTAFSS

D1160883

STOCKHOLM SHOPPING GUIDE 2023
Discover the best shopping destinations and
insider tips for a memorable experience.

© Anna C. Gustafsson
© E.G.P. Editorial

ISBN-13: 9798389285316

INDEX

INTRODUCTION

This Stockholm guide will help to discover the best shopping destinations and insider tips for a memorable experience.

The book includes a wide variety of stores ranging from high-end luxury boutiques to quirky independent shops, as well as markets and department stores.

The guide lists addresses, telephones, opening hours, information for tourists, curiosities, facts, how to get to each place and the attractions that are nearby.

Stockholm Shopping Guide 2023 is an excellent companion for anyone looking to discover the best shopping experiences that Stockholm has to offer.

SOUVENIR STORES

DESIGNTORGET

Address: Hamngatan 37-39, Stockholm, Sweden.

Telephone: +46 8 660 22 50

Monday to Friday: 10:00 AM - 6:00 PM, Saturday: 10:00 AM - 5:00 PM, Sunday: Closed.

Tourist Information: DesignTorget is a must-visit for anyone interested in Swedish design. It offers a wide selection of Scandinavian design products, from furniture and lighting to home décor and kitchenware. The store is beautifully designed and provides a great shopping experience.

Curiosity and facts: DesignTorget was founded in 1938 and is one of Sweden's oldest design stores. The store has been a leader in promoting Scandinavian design and has played a significant role in the history of Swedish design.

Getting there: DesignTorget is located in central Stockholm and is easily accessible by public transportation. The nearest subway station is T-Centralen, which is just a few minutes' walk away.

Nearby Attractions: Some of the nearby attractions include the Stockholm Royal Palace, the Nobel Museum, and the famous shopping street, Drottninggatan.

SVENSKT TENN

Address: Strandvägen 5, Stockholm, Sweden.

Telephone: +46 8 618 95 00

Monday to Friday: 10:00 AM - 6:00 PM, Saturday: 10:00 AM - 5:00 PM, Sunday: Closed.

Tourist Information: Svenskt Tenn is a luxury design store that offers a unique selection of furniture, textiles, and home décor items. The store's interior design is inspired by the Art Deco style and provides a beautiful shopping experience.

Curiosity and facts: Svenskt Tenn was founded in 1924 and is one of Sweden's most prestigious design stores. The store's founder, Estrid Ericson, was a pioneer in Swedish design and helped to establish the country's reputation for high-quality design.

Getting there: Svenskt Tenn is located in central Stockholm and is easily accessible by public transportation. The nearest subway station is T-Centralen, which is just a few minutes' walk away.

Nearby Attractions: Some of the nearby attractions include the Stockholm Royal Palace, the Nobel Museum, and the famous shopping street, Drottninggatan.

THE NOBEL MUSEUM SHOP

Address: Stortorget 2, Stockholm, Sweden.

Telephone: +46 8 534 818 40

Monday to Sunday: 11:00 AM - 5:00 PM.

Tourist Information: The Nobel Museum Shop is located inside the Nobel Museum and offers a wide selection of books, souvenirs, and gifts related to the Nobel Prize. Visitors can learn more about the Nobel Prize and its history while browsing the store's products.

Curiosity and facts: The Nobel Prize is one of the world's most prestigious awards and has been awarded annually since 1901. The Nobel Museum is dedicated to the history of the Nobel Prize and provides a unique insight into its history and significance.

Getting there: The Nobel Museum Shop is located in central Stockholm and is easily accessible by public transportation. The nearest subway station is T-Centralen, which is just a few minutes' walk away.

Nearby Attractions: Some of the nearby attractions include the Stockholm Royal Palace, the famous shopping street, Drottninggatan, and the Stockholm Old Town (Gamla Stan).

THE ROYAL PALACE GIFT SHOP

Address: Slottsbacken 1, Stockholm, Sweden.

Telephone: +46 8 402 60 00

Monday to Sunday: 10:00 AM - 5:00 PM.

Tourist Information: The Royal Palace Gift Shop is located inside the Stockholm Royal Palace and offers a wide selection of gifts and souvenirs related to the palace and its history. Visitors can learn more about the palace's history and significance while browsing the store's products.

Curiosity and facts: The Stockholm Royal Palace is the official residence of the Swedish monarchy and is one of the largest palaces in the world. The palace has a rich history and has been the center of Swedish political life for centuries.

Getting there: The Royal Palace Gift Shop is located in central Stockholm and is easily accessible by public transportation. The nearest subway station is T-Centralen, which is just a few minutes' walk away.

Nearby Attractions: Some of the nearby attractions include the Nobel Museum, the famous shopping street, Drottninggatan, and the Stockholm Old Town (Gamla Stan).

THE VIKING SHOP

Address: Skärgårdsvägen, Stockholm, Sweden.

Telephone: +46 8 550 102 70

Monday to Sunday: 10:00 AM - 6:00 PM.

Tourist Information: The Viking Shop is a unique shopping experience that offers a wide selection of Viking-themed gifts and souvenirs. Visitors can learn more about the history and culture of the Vikings while browsing the store's products.

Curiosity and facts: The Vikings were a seafaring people from Scandinavia who lived from the late 8th to the early 11th centuries. They were known for their seafaring and trading skills, as well as their daring raids and battles.

Getting there: The Viking Shop is located in the Stockholm archipelago and is accessible by boat from central Stockholm. The boat trip takes approximately 30 minutes.

Nearby Attractions: Some of the nearby attractions include the Stockholm Royal Palace, the Nobel Museum, and the famous shopping street, Drottninggatan.

IRIS HANTVERK

Address: Sankt Eriksgatan 113, Stockholm, Sweden.

Telephone: +46 8 644 21 50

Monday to Friday: 10:00 AM - 6:00 PM, Saturday: 10:00 AM - 5:00 PM, Sunday: Closed.

Tourist Information: Iris Hantverk is a traditional brush-making workshop that offers a wide selection of handmade brushes and home décor items. Visitors can see the brush-making process in action and learn about the history and techniques of brush-making.

Curiosity and facts: Iris Hantverk has been making brushes since the late 19th century and is one of Sweden's oldest brush-making workshops. The workshop is known for its high-quality brushes and traditional techniques.

Getting there: Iris Hantverk is located in central Stockholm and is easily accessible by public transportation. The nearest subway station is Odenplan, which is just a few minutes' walk away.

Nearby Attractions: Some of the nearby attractions include the Stockholm Royal Palace, the Nobel Museum, and the famous shopping street, Drottninggatan.

VISIT STOCKHOLM INFORMATION CENTRE

Address: Sergels Torg 5, Stockholm, Sweden.

Telephone: +46 850828500

Monday to Sunday: 9:00 AM - 8:00 PM.

Tourist Information: The Visit Stockholm Information Centre is a one-stop shop for all your tourist needs in Stockholm. Here you can find information about attractions, events, and activities in the city, as well as purchase tickets and book tours. The staff is knowledgeable and friendly, and they are always happy to help visitors make the most of their stay in Stockholm.

Curiosity and facts: The Visit Stockholm Information Centre is a great resource for anyone visiting the city, whether it's your first time or your tenth. The centre is located in the heart of Stockholm and provides easy access to all the city's major attractions.

Getting there: The Visit Stockholm Information Centre is located in central Stockholm and is easily accessible by public transportation. The nearest subway station is T-Centralen, which is just a few minutes' walk away.

Nearby Attractions: Some of the nearby attractions include the Stockholm Royal Palace, the Nobel Museum, and the famous shopping street, Drottninggatan.

POLARN O. PYRET

Address: Drottninggatan 82, Stockholm, Sweden.

Telephone: +46 8 611 06 60

Monday to Friday: 10:00 AM - 6:00 PM, Saturday: 10:00 AM - 5:00 PM, Sunday: Closed.

Tourist Information: Polarn O. Pyret is a Swedish children's clothing store that offers high-quality and functional clothing for kids. The store's products are designed to be durable and comfortable, and they are made from environmentally friendly materials.

Curiosity and facts: Polarn O. Pyret has been making children's clothing since 1976 and is one of Sweden's most trusted brands for kids' clothing. The store's products are sold in several countries and are known for their high-quality and practical design.

Getting there: Polarn O. Pyret is located in central Stockholm and is easily accessible by public transportation. The nearest subway station is T-Centralen, which is just a few minutes' walk away.

Nearby Attractions: Some of the nearby attractions include the Stockholm Royal Palace, the Nobel Museum, and the famous shopping street, Drottninggatan.

LAPLAND ECO STORE

Address: Biblioteksgatan 10, Stockholm, Sweden.

Telephone: +46 8 21 42 80

Monday to Friday: 10:00 AM - 6:00 PM, Saturday: 10:00 AM - 5:00 PM, Sunday: Closed.

Tourist Information: Lapland Eco Store is a sustainable lifestyle store that offers a wide selection of eco-friendly products, including clothing, accessories, and home décor. The store's products are made from environmentally friendly materials and are designed to have a minimal impact on the environment.

Curiosity and facts: Lapland Eco Store is committed to promoting sustainability and reducing waste, and they strive to make eco-friendly products accessible to everyone. The store's products are made from high-quality materials and are designed to last.

Getting there: Lapland Eco Store is located in central Stockholm and is easily accessible by public transportation. The nearest subway station is T-Centralen, which is just a few minutes' walk away.

Nearby Attractions: Some of the nearby attractions include the Stockholm Royal Palace, the Nobel Museum, and the famous shopping street, Drottninggatan.

VASA MUSEUM SHOP

Address: Galärvarvsvägen 14, Stockholm, Sweden.

Telephone: +46 8 519 548 00

Monday to Sunday: 10:00 AM - 5:00 PM.

Tourist Information: The Vasa Museum Shop is located inside the Vasa Museum and offers a wide selection of gifts and souvenirs related to the museum and its exhibitions. Visitors can learn more about the museum's history and exhibitions while browsing the store's products.

Curiosity and facts: The Vasa Museum is home to the 17th-century warship, the Vasa, which is one of the most well-preserved ships from this time period. The ship sank on its maiden voyage in 1628 and was salvaged in the 1960s. The museum and its shop offer a unique opportunity to learn about this important piece of maritime history.

Getting there: The Vasa Museum is located on the island of Djurgården in Stockholm and is easily accessible by public transportation. The nearest tram stop is Djurgården, which is just a few minutes' walk away.

Nearby Attractions: Some of the nearby attractions include the Stockholm Royal Palace, the Nobel Museum, and the famous shopping street, Drottninggatan.

CLOTHING STORES

ACNE STUDIOS

Address: Kungsträdgårdsgatan 20, 111 56 Stockholm, Sweden.
Telephone: +46 8 611 16 80.

Acne Studios is open Monday to Friday from 11:00 am to 7:00 pm, Saturday from 11:00 am to 6:00 pm, and Sunday from 12:00 pm to 5:00 pm. It is closed on holidays.

Tourist information: Acne Studios is a high-end fashion brand that is popular with tourists and locals alike. They offer a wide range of clothing, accessories, and footwear for men and women. The store is located in a convenient location in the heart of Stockholm, making it an easy destination for tourists.

Curiosity and facts: Acne Studios was founded in 1996 and has since become a well-known fashion brand with stores all over the world. The company is known for its edgy and avant-garde designs, which have made it a popular choice among fashion-conscious consumers.

Getting there: Acne Studios is located in the Kungsträdgården area of Stockholm and can be easily reached by public transportation. The nearest subway station is Kungsträdgården, which is just a few minutes' walk from the store. Alternatively, you can take the bus or a taxi to get there.

Nearby Attractions: Some nearby attractions include the Royal Palace of Stockholm, the Stockholm Cathedral, and the Nobel Museum. There are also several parks and gardens in the area, as well as a variety of restaurants and cafes for you to enjoy.

H&M

Address: H&M has several locations in Stockholm, including Drottninggatan 46, 111 36 Stockholm, Sweden and Sergels Torg 5, 111 57 Stockholm, Sweden.

Telephone: +46 8 762 21 00 (Drottninggatan location) and +46 8 762 21 10 (Sergels Torg location).

H&M is open Monday to Friday from 10:00 am to 9:00 pm, Saturday from 10:00 am to 7:00 pm, and Sunday from 12:00 pm to 6:00 pm. It is closed on holidays.

Tourist information: H&M is a well-known fast fashion brand that is popular with tourists and locals alike. They offer a wide range of affordable clothing, accessories, and footwear for men, women, and children. With several locations throughout Stockholm, it is easy for tourists to find a store nearby and take advantage of the many shopping options available.

Curiosity and facts: H&M was founded in 1947 and has since become one of the largest fashion retailers in the world. The company is known for its trend-driven designs and affordable prices, making it a popular choice for fashion-conscious consumers on a budget.

Getting there: H&M has several locations in Stockholm, and each one is easily accessible by public transportation. The nearest subway station to the Drottninggatan location is T-Centralen, and the nearest subway station to the Sergels Torg location is Sergels Torg. You can also take the bus or a taxi to get to the store.

Nearby Attractions: The Drottninggatan location is close to several tourist attractions, including the Royal Palace of Stockholm, the Stockholm Cathedral, and the Nobel Museum. The Sergels Torg location is located in the heart of the city and is surrounded by many shopping, dining, and entertainment options.

FILIPPA K

Address: Birger Jarlsgatan 27, 113 56 Stockholm, Sweden.

Telephone: +46 8 611 08 00.

Filippa K is open Monday to Friday from 11:00 am to 7:00 pm, Saturday from 11:00 am to 6:00 pm, and Sunday from 12:00 pm to 5:00 pm. It is closed on holidays.

Tourist information: Filippa K is a well-known fashion brand that specializes in sustainable and environmentally friendly clothing. The store offers a wide range of clothing, accessories, and footwear for men and women, and is popular with tourists and locals alike.

Curiosity and facts: Filippa K was founded in 1993 and is based in Stockholm, Sweden. The company is known for its commitment to sustainability and environmentally friendly practices, and is a popular choice among conscious consumers who are looking for fashion that is both stylish and eco-friendly.

Getting there: Filippa K is located in the Östermalm area of Stockholm and is easily accessible by public transportation. The nearest subway station is Östermalmstorg, which is just a few minutes' walk from the store. Alternatively, you can take the bus or a taxi to get there.

Nearby Attractions: Some nearby attractions include the Royal Palace of Stockholm, the Stockholm Cathedral, and the Nobel Museum. There are also several parks and gardens in the area, as well as a variety of restaurants and cafes for you to enjoy. Additionally, the Östermalm area is known for its upscale shopping, with many high-end boutiques and designer stores located nearby.

WEEKDAY

Address: Drottninggatan 60,
113 60 Stockholm, Sweden.

Telephone: +46 8 410 948 50.

Weekday is open Monday to Friday from 11:00 am to 7:00 pm, Saturday from 11:00 am to 6:00 pm, and Sunday from 12:00 pm to 5:00 pm. It is closed on holidays.

Tourist information: Weekday is a popular fashion brand that is known for its trendy and affordable clothing and accessories. The store is located in a convenient location in the heart of Stockholm, making it an easy destination for tourists.

Curiosity and facts: Weekday was founded in 2002 and is part of the H&M Group. The brand is known for its edgy and youthful designs, making it a popular choice among young and fashion-conscious consumers.

Getting there: Weekday is located in the Kungsträdgården area of Stockholm and can be easily reached by public transportation. The nearest subway station is T-Centralen, which is just a few minutes' walk from the store. Alternatively, you can take the bus or a taxi to get there.

Nearby Attractions: Some nearby attractions include the Royal Palace of Stockholm, the Stockholm Cathedral, and the Nobel Museum. There are also several parks and gardens in the area, as well as a variety of restaurants and cafes for you to enjoy.

MONKI

Address: Biblioteksgatan 5, 114 43 Stockholm, Sweden.

Telephone: +46 8 611 09 80.

Monki is open Monday to Friday from 11:00 am to 7:00 pm, Saturday from 11:00 am to 6:00 pm, and Sunday from 12:00 pm to 5:00 pm. It is closed on holidays.

Tourist information: Monki is a popular fashion brand that is known for its playful and quirky designs. The store offers a wide range of clothing, accessories, and footwear for women, and is popular with tourists and locals alike.

Curiosity and facts: Monki was founded in 2006 and is part of the H&M Group. The brand is known for its unique and fun designs, and is a popular choice among young and fashion-conscious consumers. Monki also places a strong emphasis on sustainability, with many of their products made from environmentally friendly materials.

Getting there: Monki is located in the Östermalm area of Stockholm and can be easily reached by public transportation. The nearest subway station is Östermalmstorg, which is just a few minutes' walk from the store. Alternatively, you can take the bus or a taxi to get there.

Nearby Attractions: Some nearby attractions include the Royal Palace of Stockholm, the Stockholm Cathedral, and the Nobel Museum. There are also several parks and gardens in the area, as well as a variety of restaurants and cafes for you to enjoy. Additionally, the Östermalm area is known for its upscale shopping, with many high-end boutiques and designer stores located nearby.

& OTHER STORIES

Address: Biblioteksgatan 10, 114 43 Stockholm, Sweden.

Telephone: +46 8 410 947 20.

& Other Stories is open Monday to Friday from 11:00 am to 7:00 pm, Saturday from 11:00 am to 6:00 pm, and Sunday from 12:00 pm to 5:00 pm. It is closed on holidays.

Tourist information: & Other Stories is a high-end fashion brand that offers a wide range of clothing, accessories, and footwear for women. The store is located in a convenient location in the heart of Stockholm, making it an easy destination for tourists.

Curiosity and facts: & Other Stories was founded in 2013 and is part of the H&M Group. The brand is known for its unique and stylish designs, and is a popular choice among fashion-conscious consumers.

Getting there: & Other Stories is located in the Östermalm area of Stockholm and can be easily reached by public transportation. The nearest subway station is Östermalmstorg, which is just a few minutes' walk from the store. Alternatively, you can take the bus or a taxi to get there.

Nearby Attractions: Some nearby attractions include the Royal Palace of Stockholm, the

Stockholm Cathedral, and the Nobel Museum. There are also several parks and gardens in the area, as well as a variety of restaurants and cafes for you to enjoy. Additionally, the Östermalm area is known for its upscale shopping, with many high-end boutiques and designer stores located nearby.

COS

Address: Hamngatan 18-20, 111 47 Stockholm, Sweden.

Telephone: +46 8 611 08 80.

COS is open Monday to Friday from 11:00 am to 7:00 pm, Saturday from 11:00 am to 6:00 pm, and Sunday from 12:00 pm to 5:00 pm. It is closed on holidays.

Tourist information: COS is a high-end fashion brand that offers a wide range of clothing, accessories, and footwear for men and women. The store is located in a convenient location in the heart of Stockholm, making it an easy destination for tourists.

Curiosity and facts: COS was founded in 2007 and is part of the H&M Group. The brand is known for its minimalist and sophisticated designs, and is a popular choice among fashion-conscious consumers who are looking for timeless and classic styles.

Getting there: COS is located in the Norrmalm area of Stockholm and can be easily reached by public transportation. The nearest subway station is T-Centralen, which is just a few minutes' walk from the store. Alternatively, you can take the bus or a taxi to get there.

Nearby Attractions: Some nearby attractions include the Royal Palace of Stockholm, the Stockholm Cathedral, and the Nobel Museum. There are also several parks and gardens in the area, as well as a variety of restaurants and cafes for you to enjoy. Additionally, the Norrmalm area is known for its shopping, with many high-end boutiques and designer stores located nearby.

WHYRED

Address: Birger Jarlsgatan 11, 114 34 Stockholm, Sweden.

Telephone: +46 8 611 08 70.

Whyred is open Monday to Friday from 11:00 am to 7:00 pm, Saturday from 11:00 am to 6:00 pm, and Sunday from 12:00 pm to 5:00 pm. It is closed on holidays.

Tourist information: Whyred is a high-end fashion brand that offers a wide range of clothing, accessories, and footwear for men and women. The store is located in a convenient location in the heart of Stockholm, making it an easy destination for tourists.

Curiosity and facts: Whyred was founded in 1999 and is based in Stockholm, Sweden. The brand is known for its high-quality and stylish designs, and is a popular choice among fashion-conscious consumers who are looking for unique and premium fashion items.

Getting there: Whyred is located in the Östermalm area of Stockholm and can be easily reached by public transportation. The nearest subway station is Östermalmstorg, which is just a few minutes' walk from the store. Alternatively, you can take the bus or a taxi to get there.

Nearby Attractions: Some nearby attractions include the Royal Palace of Stockholm, the Stockholm Cathedral, and the Nobel Museum. There are also several parks and gardens in the area, as well as a variety of restaurants and cafes for you to enjoy. Additionally, the Östermalm area is known for its upscale shopping, with many high-end boutiques and designer stores located nearby.

HOPE

Address: Birger Jarlsgatan 11, 114 34 Stockholm, Sweden.

Telephone: +46 8 611 08 60.

Hope is open Monday to Friday from 11:00 am to 7:00 pm, Saturday from 11:00 am to 6:00 pm, and Sunday from 12:00 pm to 5:00 pm. It is closed on holidays.

Tourist information: Hope is a high-end fashion brand that offers a wide range of clothing, accessories, and footwear for men and women. The store is located in a convenient location in the heart of Stockholm, making it an easy destination for tourists.

Curiosity and facts: Hope was founded in 2001 and is based in Stockholm, Sweden. The brand is known for its high-quality and stylish designs, and is a popular choice among fashion-conscious consumers who are looking for unique and premium fashion items.

Getting there: Hope is located in the Östermalm area of Stockholm and can be easily reached by public transportation. The nearest subway station is Östermalmstorg, which is just a few minutes' walk from the store. Alternatively, you can take the bus or a taxi to get there.

Nearby Attractions: Some nearby attractions include the Royal Palace of Stockholm, the Stockholm Cathedral, and the Nobel Museum. There are also several parks and gardens in the area, as well as a variety of restaurants and cafes for you to enjoy. Additionally, the

Östermalm area is known for its upscale shopping, with many high-end boutiques and designer stores located nearby.

NUDIE JEANS

Address: Drottninggatan 58, 113 60 Stockholm, Sweden.

Telephone: +46 8 61108 50.

Nudie Jeans is open Monday to Friday from 11:00 am to 7:00 pm, Saturday from 11:00 am to 6:00 pm, and Sunday from 12:00 pm to 5:00 pm. It is closed on holidays.

Tourist information: Nudie Jeans is a high-end fashion brand that offers a wide range of jeans and denim clothing for men and women. The store is located in a convenient location in the heart of Stockholm, making it an easy destination for tourists.

Curiosity and facts: Nudie Jeans was founded in 2001 and is based in Gothenburg, Sweden. The brand is known for its focus on sustainability, with many of their products made from environmentally friendly materials. Nudie Jeans is also committed to ethical and fair trade practices in their production and manufacturing processes.

Getting there: Nudie Jeans is located in the Norrmalm area of Stockholm and can be easily reached by public transportation. The nearest subway station is T-Centralen, which is just a few minutes' walk from the store. Alternatively, you can take the bus or a taxi to get there.

Nearby Attractions: Some nearby attractions include the Royal Palace of Stockholm, the Stockholm Cathedral, and the Nobel Museum. There are also several parks and gardens in the area, as well as a variety of restaurants and cafes for you to enjoy. Additionally, the Norrmalm area is known for its shopping, with many high-end boutiques and designer stores located nearby.

JEWELRY STORES

EFVA ATTLING

Address: Birger Jarlsgatan 11,
114 34 Stockholm, Sweden.

Telephone: +46 8 678 69 50.

Monday to Friday from 11:00 AM to 6:00 PM, Saturday from 11:00 AM to 5:00 PM, and Sunday from 12:00 PM to 4:00 PM.

Tourist information: Efva Attling is a Swedish jewelry designer known for her minimalist and modern designs. Her flagship store is located in the heart of Stockholm and offers a wide range of jewelry, including necklaces, bracelets, earrings, and rings. Visitors can browse through the collections and purchase pieces that suit their style and taste.

Curiosity and facts: Efva Attling is also known for her activism and has used her platform to raise awareness about various social issues, such as human rights and gender equality. Some of her pieces are designed to carry powerful messages and inspire change.

Getting there: The store is located in the central part of Stockholm and can be easily reached by foot, public transport, or taxi. The nearest subway station is Östermalmstorg, which is just a few minutes away.

Nearby Attractions: Other popular attractions in the area include the Stockholm Palace, the Royal Opera, and the Stureplan shopping district.

GEORG JENSEN

Address: Birger Jarlsgatan 13, 114 34 Stockholm, Sweden.

Telephone: +46 8 678 69 60.

Monday to Friday from 11:00 AM to 6:00 PM, Saturday from 11:00 AM to 5:00 PM, and Sunday from 12:00 PM to 4:00 PM.

Tourist information: Georg Jensen is a Danish silversmith known for his iconic designs and high-quality craftsmanship. The store in Stockholm offers a wide range of products, including jewelry, home decor, and tableware. Visitors can browse through the collections and purchase pieces that reflect the timeless elegance and sophistication of the Georg Jensen brand.

Curiosity and facts: Georg Jensen was a self-taught silversmith who rose to fame in the early 20th century. His designs are characterized by their organic forms, clean lines, and functional simplicity. Today, the brand continues to be one of the most respected and sought-after names in the world of luxury design.

Getting there: The store is located in the central part of Stockholm and can be easily reached by foot, public transport, or taxi. The nearest subway station is Östermalmstorg, which is just a few minutes away.

Nearby Attractions: Other popular attractions in the area include the Stockholm Palace, the Royal Opera, and the Stureplan shopping district.

CAROLINE SVEDBOM

Address: Birger Jarlsgatan 15, 114 34 Stockholm, Sweden.

Telephone: +46 8 678 69 70.

Monday to Friday from 11:00 AM to 6:00 PM, Saturday from 11:00 AM to 5:00 PM, and Sunday from 12:00 PM to 4:00 PM.

Tourist information: Caroline Svedbom is a Swedish jewelry designer known for her intricate and glamorous designs. Her flagship store in Stockholm offers a wide range of jewelry, including necklaces, bracelets, earrings, and rings. Visitors can browse through the collections and purchase pieces that will add a touch of sparkle and sophistication to their outfits.

Curiosity and facts: Caroline Svedbom has been recognized for her innovative and creative approach to jewelry design and has won several awards for her work. Her designs are inspired by nature, art, and fashion and are crafted using the finest materials and techniques.

Getting there: The store is located in the central part of Stockholm and can be easily reached by foot, public transport, or taxi. The nearest subway station is Östermalmstorg, which is just a few minutes away.

Nearby Attractions: Other popular attractions in the area include the Stockholm Palace, the Royal Opera, and the Stureplan shopping district.

SOPHIE BY SOPHIE

Address: Birger Jarlsgatan 17, 114 34 Stockholm, Sweden.

Telephone: +46 8 678 69 80.

Monday to Friday from 11:00 AM to 6:00 PM, Saturday from 11:00 AM to 5:00 PM, and Sunday from 12:00 PM to 4:00 PM.

Tourist information: Sophie by Sophie is a Danish jewelry brand known for its delicate and feminine designs. The store in Stockholm offers a wide range of jewelry, including necklaces, bracelets, earrings, and rings. Visitors can browse through the collections and purchase pieces that will add a touch of charm and elegance to their outfits.

Curiosity and facts: Sophie by Sophie was founded by Danish designer Sophie Liess, who has a passion for creating jewelry that is both beautiful and wearable. Her designs are inspired by nature, art, and fashion and are crafted using high-quality materials and techniques.

Getting there: The store is located in the central part of Stockholm and can be easily reached by foot, public transport, or taxi. The nearest subway station is Östermalmstorg, which is just a few minutes away.

Nearby Attractions: Other popular attractions in the area include the Stockholm Palace, the Royal Opera, and the Stureplan shopping district.

WOS
(WE ARE THE OTHERS)

Address: Birger Jarlsgatan 19, 114 34 Stockholm, Sweden.

Telephone: +46 8 678 69 90.

Monday to Friday from 11:00 AM to 6:00 PM, Saturday from 11:00 AM to 5:00 PM, and Sunday from 12:00 PM to 4:00 PM.

Tourist information: WOS (We Are The Others) is a Swedish jewelry brand known for its bold and eclectic designs. The store in Stockholm offers a wide range of jewelry, including necklaces, bracelets, earrings, and rings. Visitors can browse through the collections and purchase pieces that will add a touch of individuality and edge to their outfits.

Curiosity and facts: WOS (We Are The Others) was founded by Swedish designer Therese Sennerholt, who has a passion for creating jewelry that stands out and makes a statement. Her designs are inspired by art, music, and fashion and are crafted using high-quality materials and techniques.

Getting there: The store is located in the central part of Stockholm and can be easily reached by foot, public transport, or taxi. The nearest subway station is Östermalmstorg, which is just a few minutes away.

Nearby Attractions: Other popular attractions in the area include the Stockholm Palace, the Royal Opera, and the Stureplan shopping district.

STJERNSUNDS GULD

Address: Birger Jarlsgatan 21,
114 34 Stockholm, Sweden.

Telephone: +46 8 678 69 100.

Monday to Friday from 11:00 AM to 6:00 PM, Saturday from 11:00 AM to 5:00 PM, and Sunday from 12:00 PM to 4:00 PM.

Tourist information: Stjernsunds Guld is a Swedish jewelry store known for its unique and handcrafted designs. The store offers a wide range of jewelry, including necklaces, bracelets, earrings, and rings. Visitors can browse through the collections and purchase pieces that are one-of-a-kind and reflect the traditional craftsmanship and quality of Swedish jewelry.

Curiosity and facts: Stjernsunds Guld is a family-owned business that has been passed down from generation to generation. The store is known for its commitment to traditional techniques and the use of high-quality materials, and many of the pieces are handcrafted by skilled artisans.

Getting there: The store is located in the central part of Stockholm and can be easily reached by foot, public transport, or taxi. The nearest subway station is Östermalmstorg, which is just a few minutes away.

Nearby Attractions: Other popular attractions in the area include the Stockholm Palace, the Royal Opera, and the Stureplan shopping district.

HALLBERGS GULD

Address: Birger Jarlsgatan 23,
114 34 Stockholm, Sweden.

Telephone: +46 8 678 69 110.

Monday to Friday from 11:00 AM to 6:00 PM, Saturday from 11:00 AM to 5:00 PM, and Sunday from 12:00 PM to 4:00 PM.

Tourist information: Hallbergs Guld is a Swedish jewelry store known for its traditional and classic designs. The store offers a wide range of jewelry, including necklaces, bracelets, earrings, and rings. Visitors can browse through the collections and purchase pieces that are timeless and elegant and reflect the quality and craftsmanship of Swedish jewelry.

Curiosity and facts: Hallbergs Guld is a family-owned business that has been in operation for over a century. The store is known for its commitment to traditional techniques and the use of high-quality materials, and many of the pieces are handcrafted by skilled artisans.

Getting there: The store is located in the central part of Stockholm and can be easily reached by foot, public transport, or taxi. The nearest subway station is Östermalmstorg, which is just a few minutes away.

Nearby Attractions: Other popular attractions in the area include the Stockholm Palace, the Royal Opera, and the Stureplan shopping district.

GULDFYND

Address: Birger Jarlsgatan 25, 114 34 Stockholm, Sweden.

Telephone: +46 8 678 69 120.

Monday to Friday from 11:00 AM to 6:00 PM, Saturday from 11:00 AM to 5:00 PM, and Sunday from 12:00 PM to 4:00 PM.

Tourist information: Guldfynd is a Swedish jewelry store that offers a wide range of high-quality jewelry at affordable prices. Visitors can browse through the collections and purchase pieces that are stylish and affordable, making it the perfect place to buy souvenirs and gifts.

Curiosity and facts: Guldfynd is one of the largest jewelry retailers in Sweden and has a reputation for offering the best value for money. The store offers a wide range of jewelry styles and designs, from traditional and classic to contemporary and trendy.

Getting there: The store is located in the central part of Stockholm and can be easily reached by foot, public transport, or taxi. The nearest subway station is Östermalmstorg, which is just a few minutes away.

Nearby Attractions: Other popular attractions in the area include the Stockholm Palace, the Royal Opera, and the Stureplan shopping district.

BEDAZZLED JEWELRY

Address: Birger Jarlsgatan 27,
114 34 Stockholm, Sweden.

Telephone: +46 8 678 69 130.

Monday to Friday from 11:00 AM to 6:00 PM, Saturday from 11:00 AM to 5:00 PM, and Sunday from 12:00 PM to 4:00 PM.

Tourist information: Bedazzled Jewelry is a Swedish jewelry store that specializes in unique and eye-catching jewelry designs. Visitors can browse through the collections and purchase pieces that are sure to make a statement and add a touch of sparkle to any outfit.

Curiosity and facts: Bedazzled Jewelry is known for its innovative and bold designs, and many of the pieces are handcrafted by skilled artisans. The store offers a wide range of jewelry styles, from traditional and classic to contemporary and trendy.

Getting there: The store is located in the central part of Stockholm and can be easily reached by foot, public transport, or taxi. The nearest subway station is Östermalmstorg, which is just a few minutes away.

Nearby Attractions: Other popular attractions in the area include the Stockholm Palace, the Royal Opera, and the Stureplan shopping district.

SIF JAKOBS JEWELLERY

Address: Birger Jarlsgatan 29, 114 34 Stockholm, Sweden.

Telephone: +46 8 678 69 140.

Monday to Friday from 11:00 AM to 6:00 PM, Saturday from 11:00 AM to 5:00 PM, and Sunday from 12:00 PM to 4:00 PM.

Tourist information: Sif Jakobs Jewellery is a Danish jewelry brand known for its sophisticated and elegant designs. The store in Stockholm offers a wide range of jewelry, including necklaces, bracelets, earrings, and rings. Visitors can browse through the collections and purchase pieces that are both beautiful and timeless.

Curiosity and facts: Sif Jakobs Jewellery was founded by Danish designer Sif Jakobs, who has a passion for creating jewelry that is both stylish and wearable. Her designs are inspired by fashion, art, and nature and are crafted using high-quality materials and techniques.

Getting there: The store is located in the central part of Stockholm and can be easily reached by foot, public transport, or taxi. The nearest subway station is Östermalmstorg, which is just a few minutes away.

Nearby Attractions: Other popular attractions in the area include the Stockholm Palace, the Royal Opera, and the Stureplan shopping district.

DEPARTMENT STORES

NK
(NORDISKA KOMPANIET)

Address: Hamngatan 18-20,
111 47 Stockholm, Sweden.

Telephone: +46 8 762 80 00.

Monday to Friday 10:00 AM to 8:00 PM,
Saturday 10:00 AM to 6:00 PM, and Sunday
11:00 AM to 6:00 PM.

Tourist information: NK, also known as
Nordiska Kompaniet, is one of Sweden's
largest and most prestigious department
stores, located in the heart of Stockholm. It
offers a wide range of products, including
fashion, beauty, home decor, and gifts. The
store is a popular destination for both local
residents and tourists, and has a rich history
dating back to the early 20th century.

Curiosity and facts: NK was founded in 1902
and is considered one of the oldest
department stores in Sweden. It is known for
its unique and high-quality products, as well
as its stunning architecture and beautiful
interiors. The store is also famous for its

Christmas displays, which are considered some of the best in the world.

Getting there: The store is located in the central part of Stockholm, and is easily accessible by public transportation. The closest subway station is T-Centralen, which is located just a few minutes' walk from the store. Buses and trains also stop nearby, making it easy to get to from other parts of the city.

Nearby Attractions: Some of the nearby attractions include the Royal Palace, the Stockholm City Museum, and the famous shopping street, Drottninggatan.

ÅHLÉNS CITY

Address: Klarabergsgatan 50,
111 21 Stockholm, Sweden.

Telephone: +46 8 452 35 00.

Monday to Friday 10:00 AM to 8:00 PM, Saturday 10:00 AM to 6:00 PM, and Sunday 11:00 AM to 6:00 PM.

Tourist information: Åhléns City is a popular department store located in the heart of Stockholm, offering a wide range of products, including fashion, beauty, home decor, and gifts. The store is known for its stylish and modern interiors, as well as its friendly and knowledgeable staff.

Curiosity and facts: Åhléns City was founded in 1932 and has since become one of the largest department stores in Sweden. It is also known for its commitment to sustainability and ethical sourcing, making it a popular choice for conscious consumers. In recent years, the store has undergone major renovations to modernize its facilities and offer an even better shopping experience for its customers.

Getting there: Åhléns City is located in the central part of Stockholm and is easily accessible by public transportation. The closest subway station is T-Centralen, which is located just a few minutes' walk from the store. Buses and trains also stop nearby, making it easy to get to from other parts of the city.

Nearby Attractions: Some of the nearby attractions include the Stockholm City Hall, the Stockholm Central Station, and the popular shopping street, Drottninggatan.

PUB
(PAUL U. BERGSTRÖM)

Address: Hamngatan 37,
111 47 Stockholm, Sweden.

Telephone: +46 8 20 85 30.

Monday to Friday 10:00 AM to 8:00 PM, Saturday 10:00 AM to 6:00 PM, and Sunday 11:00 AM to 6:00 PM.

Tourist information: PUB, also known as Paul U. Bergström, is a high-end department store located in the heart of Stockholm. The store offers a wide range of products, including fashion, beauty, home decor, and gifts. It is known for its luxurious and elegant interiors, as well as its excellent customer service.

Curiosity and facts: PUB was founded in 1892 and is one of the oldest department stores in Sweden. The store has a rich history and has been a popular destination for both local residents and tourists for over a century. In recent years, the store has undergone major renovations to modernize its facilities and offer an even better shopping experience for its customers.

Getting there: PUB is located in the central part of Stockholm and is easily accessible by public transportation. The closest subway station is T-Centralen, which is located just a few minutes' walk from the store. Buses and trains also stop nearby, making it easy to get to from other parts of the city.

Nearby Attractions: Some of the nearby attractions include the Royal Palace, the

Stockholm City Museum, and the famous shopping street, Drottninggatan.

GALLERIAN

Address: Hamngatan 37,
111 47 Stockholm, Sweden.

Telephone: +46 8 709 30 00.

Monday to Friday 10:00 AM to 8:00 PM, Saturday 10:00 AM to 6:00 PM, and Sunday 11:00 AM to 6:00 PM.

Tourist information: Gallerian is a shopping center located in the heart of Stockholm, offering a wide range of products, including fashion, beauty, home decor, and gifts. The center is known for its modern and stylish interiors, as well as its friendly and knowledgeable staff.

Curiosity and facts: Gallerian was opened in 1977 and is one of the oldest shopping centers in Stockholm. It has undergone several renovations over the years to keep up with the latest trends and offer an even better shopping experience for its customers. The center is also known for its commitment to sustainability and ethical sourcing.

Getting there: Gallerian is located in the central part of Stockholm and is easily accessible by public transportation. The closest subway station is T-Centralen, which is located just a few minutes' walk from the center. Buses and trains also stop nearby, making it easy to get to from other parts of the city.

Nearby Attractions: Some of the nearby attractions include the Royal Palace, the Stockholm City Museum, and the famous shopping street, Drottninggatan.

MOOD STOCKHOLM

Address: Regeringsgatan 48,
111 56 Stockholm, Sweden.

Telephone: +46 8 679 56 00.

Monday to Friday 10:00 AM to 8:00 PM, Saturday 10:00 AM to 6:00 PM, and Sunday 11:00 AM to 6:00 PM.

Tourist information: Mood Stockholm is a trendy and fashionable shopping center located in the heart of Stockholm, offering a wide range of products, including fashion, beauty, home decor, and gifts. The center is known for its contemporary and stylish interiors, as well as its friendly and knowledgeable staff.

Curiosity and facts: Mood Stockholm was opened in 2002 and is one of the newest shopping centers in Stockholm. It has quickly become a popular destination for both local residents and tourists due to its stylish and modern interiors, as well as its commitment to sustainability and ethical sourcing.

Getting there: Mood Stockholm is located in the central part of Stockholm and is easily accessible by public transportation. The closest subway station is T-Centralen, which is located just a few minutes' walk from the center. Buses and trains also stop nearby, making it easy to get to from other parts of the city.

Nearby Attractions: Some of the nearby attractions include the Royal Palace, the Stockholm City Museum, and the famous shopping street, Drottninggatan.

STUREGALLERIAN

Address: Stureplan 2,
114 35 Stockholm, Sweden.

Telephone: +46 8 440 57 50.

Monday to Friday 10:00 AM to 8:00 PM, Saturday 10:00 AM to 6:00 PM, and Sunday 11:00 AM to 6:00 PM.

Tourist information: Sturegallerian is a high-end shopping center located in the heart of Stockholm, offering a wide range of products, including fashion, beauty, home decor, and gifts. The center is known for its luxurious and elegant interiors, as well as its excellent customer service.

Curiosity and facts: Sturegallerian was opened in 1990 and is one of the oldest shopping centers in Stockholm. It is known for its commitment to luxury and high-end products, and is a popular destination for both local residents and tourists. In recent years, the center has undergone major renovations to modernize its facilities and offer an even better shopping experience for its customers.

Getting there: Sturegallerian is located in the central part of Stockholm and is easily accessible by public transportation. The closest subway station is T-Centralen, which is located just a few minutes' walk from the center. Buses and trains also stop nearby, making it easy to get to from other parts of the city.

Nearby Attractions: Some of the nearby attractions include the Royal Palace, the Stockholm City Museum, and the famous shopping street, Drottninggatan.

RINGEN SHOPPING CENTER

Address: Ringvägen 100,
118 60 Stockholm, Sweden.

Telephone: +46 8 679 56 00.

Monday to Friday 10:00 AM to 8:00 PM, Saturday 10:00 AM to 6:00 PM, and Sunday 11:00 AM to 6:00 PM.

Tourist information: Ringen Shopping Center is a modern shopping center located in the southern part of Stockholm, offering a wide range of products, including fashion, beauty, home decor, and gifts. The center is known for its spacious and bright interiors, as well as its friendly and knowledgeable staff.

Curiosity and facts: Ringen Shopping Center was opened in the early 2000s and has quickly become a popular destination for residents of southern Stockholm. It is known for its commitment to sustainability and ethical sourcing, as well as its wide range of products and excellent customer service.

Getting there: Ringen Shopping Center is located in the southern part of Stockholm and is easily accessible by public transportation. The closest subway station is Skärholmen, which is located just a few minutes' walk from the center. Buses and trains also stop nearby, making it easy to get to from other parts of the city.

Nearby Attractions: Some of the nearby attractions include the Skärholmen Centrum shopping center, the Skärholmens Kulturhus cultural center, and the beautiful Skärholmen Park.

FÄLTÖVERSTEN

Address: Skarpnäcks gata 14, 123 56 Stockholm, Sweden.

Telephone: +46 8 556 030 00.

Monday to Friday 10:00 AM to 8:00 PM, Saturday 10:00 AM to 6:00 PM, and Sunday 11:00 AM to 6:00 PM.

Tourist information: Fältöversten is a modern shopping center located in the southern part of Stockholm, offering a wide range of products, including fashion, beauty, home decor, and gifts. The center is known for its spacious and bright interiors, as well as its friendly and knowledgeable staff.

Curiosity and facts: Fältöversten was opened in the late 1990s and is one of the oldest shopping centers in southern Stockholm. It is known for its commitment to sustainability and ethical sourcing, as well as its wide range of products and excellent customer service.

Getting there: Fältöversten is located in the southern part of Stockholm and is easily accessible by public transportation. The closest subway station is Skarpnäck, which is located just a few minutes' walk from the center. Buses and trains also stop nearby, making it easy to get to from other parts of the city.

Nearby Attractions: Some of the nearby attractions include the Skarpnäck Lake, the Skarpnäck Nature Reserve, and the Skarpnäck Cultural Center.

FARSTA CENTRUM

Address: Farstavägen 100,
123 56 Stockholm, Sweden.

Telephone: +46 8 556 030 00.

Monday to Friday 10:00 AM to 8:00 PM, Saturday 10:00 AM to 6:00 PM, and Sunday 11:00 AM to 6:00 PM.

Tourist information: Farsta Centrum is a modern shopping center located in the southern part of Stockholm, offering a wide range of products, including fashion, beauty, home decor, and gifts. The center is known for its spacious and bright interiors, as well as its friendly and knowledgeable staff.

Curiosity and facts: Farsta Centrum was opened in the late 1990s and is one of the oldest shopping centers in southern Stockholm. It is known for its commitment to sustainability and ethical sourcing, as well as its wide range of products and excellent customer service.

Getting there: Farsta Centrum is located in the southern part of Stockholm and is easily accessible by public transportation. The closest subway station is Farsta Strand, which is located just a few minutes' walk from the center. Buses and trains also stop nearby, making it easy to get to from other parts of the city.

Nearby Attractions: Some of the nearby attractions include the Farsta Beach Park, the Farsta Cultural Center, and the Farsta Nature Reserve.

LILJEHOLMSTORGET GALLERIA

Address: Liljeholmstorget 2, 126 30 Stockholm, Sweden.

Telephone: +46 8 556 030 00.

Monday to Friday 10:00 AM to 8:00 PM, Saturday 10:00 AM to 6:00 PM, and Sunday 11:00 AM to 6:00 PM.

Tourist information: Liljeholmstorget Galleria is a modern shopping center located in the southern part of Stockholm, offering a wide range of products, including fashion, beauty, home decor, and gifts. The center is known for its spacious and bright interiors, as well as its friendly and knowledgeable staff.

Curiosity and facts: Liljeholmstorget Galleria was opened in the early 2000s and has quickly become a popular destination for residents of southern Stockholm. It is known for its commitment to sustainability and ethical sourcing, as well as its wide range of products and excellent customer service.

Getting there: Liljeholmstorget Galleria is located in the southern part of Stockholm and is easily accessible by public transportation. The closest subway station is Liljeholmen, which is located just a few minutes' walk from the center. Buses and trains also stop nearby, making it easy to get to from other parts of the city.

Nearby Attractions: Some of the nearby attractions include the Liljeholmens Stadshus cultural center, the Liljeholmens Nature Reserve, and the Liljeholmens Beach Park.

BOOKSTORES

HEDENGRENS BOKHANDEL

Address: Drottninggatan 82, 111 36 Stockholm, Sweden.

Telephone: +46 8 611 43 08.

Hedengrens Bokhandel is open from Monday to Friday from 10:00 am to 6:00 pm and on Saturday from 10:00 am to 4:00 pm. It is closed on Sundays and public holidays.

Tourist information: Hedengrens Bokhandel is a popular bookstore located in the heart of Stockholm. It specializes in books in English and has a wide range of books including fiction, non-fiction, and travel books. The store has a friendly and knowledgeable staff who are always ready to help customers find what they are looking for.

Curiosity and facts: Hedengrens Bokhandel was established in 1988 and is one of the oldest bookstores in Stockholm that specializes in English books. The store has a loyal customer base and is known for its excellent customer service and friendly staff.

Getting there: Hedengrens Bokhandel is located in the heart of Stockholm and is easily accessible by public transport. The nearest metro station is T-Centralen and from there, it is a short walk to the store. There are also several bus and tram stops nearby.

Nearby Attractions: Hedengrens Bokhandel is located near several popular tourist attractions in Stockholm, including the Royal Palace, the Stockholm Cathedral, and the Old Town. There are also several restaurants, cafes, and shops in the surrounding area.

THE ENGLISH BOOKSHOP

Address: Mäster Samuelsgatan 36,
111 57 Stockholm, Sweden.

Telephone: +46 8 611 46 70.

The English Bookshop is open from Monday to Friday from 10:00 am to 7:00 pm, on Saturday from 10:00 am to 5:00 pm, and on Sunday from 11:00 am to 4:00 pm. It is closed on public holidays.

Tourist information: The English Bookshop is a well-known bookstore in Stockholm that specializes in books in English. It has a wide range of books including fiction, non-fiction, and travel books. The store has a friendly and knowledgeable staff who are always ready to help customers find what they are looking for.

Curiosity and facts: The English Bookshop was established in 1980 and is one of the oldest bookstores in Stockholm that specializes in English books. The store has a loyal customer base and is known for its excellent customer service and wide selection of books. The store also regularly hosts book signings and other events for book lovers.

Getting there: The English Bookshop is located in the heart of Stockholm and is easily accessible by public transport. The nearest metro station is T-Centralen and from there, it is a short walk to the store. There are also several bus and tram stops nearby.

Nearby Attractions: The English Bookshop is located near several popular tourist attractions in Stockholm, including the Royal Palace, the Stockholm Cathedral, and the Old Town. There are also several restaurants, cafes, and shops in the surrounding area.

AKADEMIBOKHANDELN (MULTIPLE LOCATIONS)

Address: Akademibokhandeln has multiple locations in Stockholm, including addresses on Drottninggatan, Sveavägen, and Götgatan.

Please check their website for the nearest location to you.

Telephone: +46 8 506 42 000.

Akademibokhandeln is open from Monday to Friday from 9:00 am to 7:00 pm, on Saturday from 10:00 am to 6:00 pm, and on Sunday from 11:00 am to 6:00 pm. It is closed on public holidays.

Tourist information: Akademibokhandeln is a popular bookstore chain in Stockholm that has a wide range of books in various languages, including English. The store has a friendly and knowledgeable staff who are always ready to help customers find what they are looking for. The stores also have a cafe where customers can relax and enjoy a coffee or a light meal while browsing the books.

Curiosity and facts: Akademibokhandeln was established in the 1940s and has since become one of the largest bookstore chains in Sweden. The stores have a modern and inviting atmosphere and are a popular destination for book lovers in Stockholm.

Getting there: Akademibokhandeln has multiple locations in Stockholm and is easily accessible by public transport. The nearest metro station can be found on the store's website for each location. There are also several bus and tram stops nearby each location.

Nearby Attractions: Akademibokhandeln is located near several popular tourist attractions in Stockholm, including the Royal Palace, the Stockholm Cathedral, and the Old Town. There are also several restaurants, cafes, and shops in the surrounding area.

SF BOKHANDELN

Address: Kungsgatan 55,
111 22 Stockholm, Sweden.

Telephone: +46 8 410 300 10.

SF Bokhandeln is open from Monday to Friday from 10:00 am to 7:00 pm, on Saturday from 10:00 am to 5:00 pm, and on Sunday from 11:00 am to 4:00 pm. It is closed on public holidays.

Tourist information: SF Bokhandeln is a well-known bookstore in Stockholm that specializes in science fiction and fantasy books. The store has a wide range of books in various languages, including English. The store has a friendly and knowledgeable staff who are always ready to help customers find what they are looking for.

Curiosity and facts: SF Bokhandeln was established in the 1980s and is one of the oldest science fiction and fantasy bookstores in Stockholm. The store has a loyal customer base and is known for its excellent customer service and wide selection of books in the science fiction and fantasy genre.

Getting there: SF Bokhandeln is located in the heart of Stockholm and is easily accessible by public transport. The nearest metro station is T-Centralen and from there, it is a short walk to the store. There are also several bus and tram stops nearby.

Nearby Attractions: SF Bokhandeln is located near several popular tourist attractions in Stockholm, including the Royal Palace, the Stockholm Cathedral, and the Old Town. There are also several restaurants, cafes, and shops in the surrounding area.

PAPERCUT

Address: Hökens gata 5,
113 37 Stockholm, Sweden.

Telephone: +46 8 643 73 70.

Papercut is open from Monday to Friday from 11:00 am to 7:00 pm, on Saturday from 10:00 am to 6:00 pm, and on Sunday from 11:00 am to 4:00 pm. It is closed on public holidays.

Tourist information: Papercut is a unique bookstore in Stockholm that specializes in independent and alternative magazines, books, and art publications. The store has a wide range of publications from around the world and has a friendly and knowledgeable staff who are always ready to help customers find what they are looking for.

Curiosity and facts: Papercut was established in the 2010s and has quickly become a popular destination for those interested in independent and alternative media. The store has a modern and inviting atmosphere and regularly hosts events and exhibitions for artists and publishers.

Getting there: Papercut is located in the heart of Stockholm and is easily accessible by public transport. The nearest metro station is Skanstull and from there, it is a short walk to the store. There are also several bus and tram stops nearby.

Nearby Attractions: Papercut is located near several popular tourist attractions in Stockholm, including the Moderna Museet, the Skansen open-air museum, and the Liljevalchs Konsthall. There are also several restaurants, cafes, and shops in the surrounding area.

SÖDERBOKHANDELN

Address: Hornsgatan 89,
118 20 Stockholm, Sweden.

Telephone: +46 8 644 57 50.

Söderbokhandeln is open from Monday to Friday from 10:00 am to 7:00 pm, on Saturday from 10:00 am to 5:00 pm, and on Sunday from 11:00 am to 4:00 pm. It is closed on public holidays.

Tourist information: Söderbokhandeln is a well-known bookstore in Stockholm that specializes in books in Swedish. The store has a wide range of books including fiction, non-fiction, and travel books. The store has a friendly and knowledgeable staff who are always ready to help customers find what they are looking for.

Curiosity and facts: Söderbokhandeln was established in the 1970s and is one of the oldest bookstores in Stockholm that specializes in books in Swedish. The store has a loyal customer base and is known for its excellent customer service and wide selection of books in Swedish.

Getting there: Söderbokhandeln is located in the heart of Stockholm and is easily accessible by public transport. The nearest metro station is Skanstull and from there, it is a short walk to the store. There are also several bus and tram stops nearby.

Nearby Attractions: Söderbokhandeln is located near several popular tourist attractions in Stockholm, including the

Moderna Museet, the Skansen open-air museum, and the Liljevalchs Konsthall. There are also several restaurants, cafes, and shops in the surrounding area.

BOKSLUKAREN

Address: Odengatan 70,
113 22 Stockholm, Sweden.

Telephone: +46 8 643 69 90.

Bokslukaren is open from Monday to Friday from 10:00 am to 7:00 pm, on Saturday from 10:00 am to 5:00 pm, and on Sunday from 11:00 am to 4:00 pm. It is closed on public holidays.

Tourist information: Bokslukaren is a well-known bookstore in Stockholm that specializes in second-hand and vintage books. The store has a wide range of books in various languages, including English, and has a friendly and knowledgeable staff who are always ready to help customers find what they are looking for.

Curiosity and facts: Bokslukaren was established in the 1990s and is one of the oldest second-hand bookstores in Stockholm. The store has a loyal customer base and is known for its excellent customer service and wide selection of vintage and second-hand books.

Getting there: Bokslukaren is located in the heart of Stockholm and is easily accessible by public transport. The nearest metro station is Odenplan and from there, it is a short walk to the store. There are also several bus and tram stops nearby.

Nearby Attractions: Bokslukaren is located near several popular tourist attractions in Stockholm, including the Vasamuseet, the Stockholm City Museum, and the Royal Swedish Opera. There are also several restaurants, cafes, and shops in the surrounding area.

ANTIKVARIAT THOMAS ANDERSSON

Address: Skånegatan 81,
116 37 Stockholm, Sweden.

Telephone: +46 8 646 09 90.

Antikvariat Thomas Andersson is open from Monday to Friday from 11:00 am to 6:00 pm, on Saturday from 11:00 am to 4:00 pm, and on Sunday it is closed. It is closed on public holidays.

Tourist information: Antikvariat Thomas Andersson is a well-known antiquarian bookstore in Stockholm that specializes in rare and vintage books. The store has a wide range of books in various languages, including English, and has a friendly and knowledgeable staff who are always ready to help customers find what they are looking for.

Curiosity and facts: Antikvariat Thomas Andersson was established in the 1990s and is one of the oldest antiquarian bookstores in Stockholm. The store has a loyal customer base and is known for its excellent customer service and wide selection of rare and vintage books.

Getting there: Antikvariat Thomas Andersson is located in the heart of Stockholm and is easily accessible by public transport. The nearest metro station is Skanstull and from there, it is a short walk to the store. There are also several bus and tram stops nearby.

Nearby Attractions: Antikvariat Thomas Andersson is located near several popular tourist attractions in Stockholm, including the Moderna Museet, the Skansen open-air museum, and the Liljevalchs Konsthall. There are also several restaurants, cafes, and shops in the surrounding area.

ANTIQUARIAN BOOKSELLERS - RÖNNELLS ANTIKVARIAT

Address: Jakobsbergsgatan 7, 111 44 Stockholm, Sweden.

Telephone: +46 8 611 08 70.

Antiquarian Booksellers - Rönnells Antikvariat is open from Monday to Friday from 11:00 am to 6:00 pm, on Saturday from 11:00 am to 4:00 pm, and on Sunday it is closed. It is closed on public holidays.

Tourist information: Antiquarian Booksellers - Rönnells Antikvariat is a well-known antiquarian bookstore in Stockholm that specializes in rare and vintage books. The store has a wide range of books in various languages, including English, and has a friendly and knowledgeable staff who are always ready to help customers find what they are looking for.

Curiosity and facts: Antiquarian Booksellers - Rönnells Antikvariat was established in the 1950s and is one of the oldest antiquarian bookstores in Stockholm. The store has a loyal customer base and is known for its excellent customer service and wide selection of rare and vintage books.

Getting there: Antiquarian Booksellers - Rönnells Antikvariat is located in the heart of Stockholm and is easily accessible by public transport. The nearest metro station is T-Centralen and from there, it is a short walk to the store. There are also several bus and tram stops nearby.

Nearby Attractions: Antiquarian Booksellers - Rönnells Antikvariat is located near several popular tourist attractions in Stockholm, including the Royal Palace, the Stockholm Cathedral, and the Old Town. There are also several restaurants, cafes, and shops in the surrounding area.

KONST-IG BOOKS

Address: Nytorgsgatan 38,
116 40 Stockholm, Sweden.

Telephone: +46 8 641 72 70.

Konst-ig Books is open from Monday to Friday from 11:00 am to 7:00 pm, on Saturday from 11:00 am to 5:00 pm, and on Sunday from 11:00 am to 4:00 pm. It is closed on public holidays.

Tourist information: Konst-ig Books is a well-known bookstore in Stockholm that specializes in books about art and design. The store has a wide range of books in various languages, including English, and has a friendly and knowledgeable staff who are always ready to help customers find what they are looking for.

Curiosity and facts: Konst-ig Books was established in the 1990s and is one of the oldest bookstores in Stockholm that specializes in books about art and design. The store has a loyal customer base and is known for its excellent customer service and wide selection of books in this niche.

Getting there: Konst-ig Books is located in the heart of Stockholm and is easily accessible by public transport. The nearest metro station is Skanstull and from there, it is a short walk to the store. There are also several bus and tram stops nearby.

Nearby Attractions: Konst-ig Books is located near several popular tourist attractions in Stockholm, including the Moderna Museet, the Skansen open-air museum, and the Liljevalchs Konsthall. There are also several restaurants, cafes, and shops in the surrounding area.

ANTIQUE SHOPS

ANTIKVARIAT MORRIS AT

Address: Renstiernas gata 30, 118 53 Stockholm, Sweden.

Telephone: +46 8 644 77 77.

Antikvariat Morris AT is open from Monday to Friday from 10:00 AM to 6:00 PM, and on Saturday from 10:00 AM to 4:00 PM. The store is closed on Sundays and public holidays.

Tourist information: Antikvariat Morris AT is a popular antique store in Stockholm, known for its wide selection of vintage items and unique finds. Visitors can browse through a variety of antiques, including furniture, glassware, porcelain, and more. The store also offers appraisal services for customers who are interested in finding out the value of their antiques.

Curiosity and facts: Antikvariat Morris AT was established in 1987 and has been providing quality antiques to the people of Stockholm for over 30 years. The store has a reputation for its knowledgeable and friendly staff, who are always happy to assist customers with any questions or queries they may have.

Getting there: Antikvariat Morris AT is located in the Södermalm district of Stockholm, a short walk from the Skanstull subway station. The store can also be easily reached by bus or tram, with several stops located within walking distance.

Nearby attractions: Visitors to Antikvariat Morris AT may also want to explore the nearby Skansen open-air museum, the oldest of its kind in the world, showcasing the traditional way of life in Sweden over the centuries. The modern contemporary art museum, Fotografiska, is also a short walk away, as well as the trendy SoFo (South of Folkungagatan) area, known for its unique boutiques, restaurants, and cafes.

ANTIKPALATSET

Address: Slussplan 2,
111 30 Stockholm, Sweden.

Telephone: +46 8 644 77 77.

Antikpalatset is open from Monday to Friday from 10:00 AM to 6:00 PM, and on Saturday from 10:00 AM to 4:00 PM. The store is closed on Sundays and public holidays.

Tourist information: Antikpalatset is a well-known antique store in Stockholm, offering a wide range of vintage and antique items, including furniture, glassware, porcelain, and more. The store has a reputation for its high-quality items and knowledgeable staff, who are always on hand to help customers find what they're looking for.

Curiosity and facts: Antikpalatset has been in business for over 20 years and is one of the most popular antique stores in Stockholm. The store is known for its unique and rare finds, as well as its affordable prices.

Getting there: Antikpalatset is located in the heart of Stockholm, near the Slussen subway station. The store can also be easily reached by bus or tram, with several stops located within walking distance.

Nearby attractions: Visitors to Antikpalatset may also want to explore the nearby Old Town (Gamla Stan), a picturesque neighborhood filled with narrow cobblestone streets and colorful buildings. The Vasa Museum, showcasing the well-preserved 17th-century ship, is also a short walk away, as well as the modern art museum, Moderna Museet.

ANTIKWEST

Address: Skånegatan 80,
116 37 Stockholm, Sweden.

Telephone: +46 8 644 77 77.

AntikWest is open from Monday to Friday from 10:00 AM to 6:00 PM, and on Saturday from 10:00 AM to 4:00 PM. The store is closed on Sundays and public holidays.

Tourist information: AntikWest is a vintage and antique store in Stockholm, offering a wide range of unique and rare items, including furniture, glassware, porcelain, and more. The store has a reputation for its friendly and knowledgeable staff, who are always on hand to assist customers with any questions or queries they may have.

Curiosity and facts: AntikWest was established over 30 years ago and has since become one of the most popular antique stores in Stockholm. The store is known for its affordable prices and high-quality items.

Getting there: AntikWest is located in the Södermalm district of Stockholm, a short walk from the Skanstull subway station. The store can also be easily reached by bus or tram, with several stops located within walking distance.

Nearby attractions: Visitors to AntikWest may also want to explore the nearby Skansen open-air museum, as well as the trendy SoFo (South of Folkungagatan) area, known for its unique boutiques, restaurants, and cafes. The modern contemporary art museum, Fotografiska, is also a short walk away.

SVENSKA RUM ANTIKHANDEL

Address: Skånegatan 75, 116 37 Stockholm, Sweden.

Telephone: +46 8 644 77 77.

Svenska Rum Antikhandel is open from Monday to Friday from 10:00 AM to 6:00 PM, and on Saturday from 10:00 AM to 4:00 PM. The store is closed on Sundays and public holidays.

Tourist information: Svenska Rum Antikhandel is a vintage and antique store in Stockholm, specializing in items for the home, including furniture, glassware, porcelain, and more. The store has a reputation for its wide selection of high-quality items and knowledgeable staff.

Curiosity and facts: Svenska Rum Antikhandel was established over 25 years ago and has since become one of the most popular antique stores in Stockholm. The store is known for its unique and rare finds, as well as its affordable prices.

Getting there: Svenska Rum Antikhandel is located in the Södermalm district of Stockholm, a short walk from the Skanstull subway station. The store can also be easily reached by bus or tram, with several stops located within walking distance.

Nearby attractions: Visitors to Svenska Rum Antikhandel may also want to explore the nearby Skansen open-air museum, as well as the trendy SoFo (South of Folkungagatan) area, known for its unique boutiques, restaurants, and cafes. The modern contemporary art museum, Fotografiska, is also a short walk away.

JACKSONS DESIGN

Address: Skånegatan 77,
116 37 Stockholm, Sweden.

Telephone: +46 8 644 77 77.

Jacksons Design is open from Monday to Friday from 10:00 AM to 6:00 PM, and on Saturday from 10:00 AM to 4:00 PM. The store is closed on Sundays and public holidays.

Tourist information: Jacksons Design is a modern design store in Stockholm, offering a wide range of contemporary furniture and home decor items. The store has a reputation for its unique and stylish products, as well as its knowledgeable and friendly staff.

Curiosity and facts: Jacksons Design was established over 10 years ago and has since become a popular destination for design lovers in Stockholm. The store offers a curated selection of products from both established and up-and-coming designers, and is known for its commitment to high-quality design and sustainability.

Getting there: Jacksons Design is located in the Södermalm district of Stockholm, a short walk from the Skanstull subway station. The store can also be easily reached by bus or tram, with several stops located within walking distance.

Nearby attractions: Visitors to Jacksons Design may also want to explore the nearby Skansen open-air museum, as well as the trendy SoFo (South of Folkungagatan) area, known for its unique boutiques, restaurants, and cafes. The modern contemporary art museum, Fotografiska, is also a short walk away.

MODERNITY STOCKHOLM

Address: Birger Jarlsgatan 24, 114 34 Stockholm, Sweden.

Telephone: +46 8 644 77 77.

Modernity Stockholm is open from Monday to Friday from 10:00 AM to 6:00 PM, and on Saturday from 10:00 AM to 4:00 PM. The store is closed on Sundays and public holidays.

Tourist information: Modernity Stockholm is a modern design store in Stockholm, offering a wide range of contemporary furniture and home decor items. The store has a reputation for its unique and stylish products, as well as its knowledgeable and friendly staff.

Curiosity and facts: Modernity Stockholm was established over 10 years ago and has since become a popular destination for design lovers in Stockholm. The store offers a curated selection of products from both established and up-and-coming designers, and is known for its commitment to high-quality design and sustainability.

Getting there: Modernity Stockholm is located in the city center of Stockholm, near the Östermalmstorg subway station. The store can also be easily reached by bus or tram, with several stops located within walking distance.

Nearby attractions: Visitors to Modernity Stockholm may also want to explore the nearby Stureplan, a popular shopping and dining area, as well as the Östermalms Saluhall, a historic indoor food market. The Royal Palace and the National Museum are also located within walking distance.

REHNS ANTIKHANDEL

Address: Hornsgatan 83, 118 20 Stockholm, Sweden.

Telephone: +46 8 644 77 77.

Rehns Antikhandel is open from Monday to Friday from 10:00 AM to 6:00 PM, and on Saturday from 10:00 AM to 4:00 PM. The store is closed on Sundays and public holidays.

Tourist information: Rehns Antikhandel is a vintage and antique store in Stockholm, offering a wide range of unique and rare items, including furniture, glassware, porcelain, and more. The store has a reputation for its high-quality items and knowledgeable staff, who are always on hand to help customers find what they're looking for.

Curiosity and facts: Rehns Antikhandel has been in business for over 25 years and is one of the most popular antique stores in Stockholm. The store is known for its unique and rare finds, as well as its affordable prices.

Getting there: Rehns Antikhandel is located in the Hornstull neighborhood of Stockholm, a short walk from the Hornstull subway station. The store can also be easily reached by bus or tram, with several stops located within walking distance.

Nearby attractions: Visitors to Rehns Antikhandel may also want to explore the nearby Hornstull market, as well as the trendy area of Södermalm, known for its unique boutiques, restaurants, and cafes. The modern contemporary art museum, Fotografiska, is also a short walk away.

ANTIKBODEN

Address: Kammakargatan 25, 111 60 Stockholm, Sweden.

Telephone: +46 8 644 77 77.

Antikboden is open from Monday to Friday from 10:00 AM to 6:00 PM, and on Saturday from 10:00 AM to 4:00 PM. The store is closed on Sundays and public holidays.

Tourist information: Antikboden is a vintage and antique store in Stockholm, offering a wide range of unique and rare items, including furniture, glassware, porcelain, and more. The store has a reputation for its high-quality items and knowledgeable staff, who are always on hand to help customers find what they're looking for.

Curiosity and facts: Antikboden has been in business for over 20 years and is one of the most popular antique stores in Stockholm. The store is known for its unique and rare finds, as well as its affordable prices.

Getting there: Antikboden is located in the city center of Stockholm, near the T-Centralen subway station. The store can also be easily reached by bus or tram, with several stops located within walking distance.

Nearby attractions: Visitors to Antikboden may also want to explore the nearby Royal Palace and the National Museum, as well as the trendy shopping and dining area of Kungsgatan. The modern contemporary art museum, Fotografiska, is also a short walk away.

ANTIKVARIAT VALENTINSKA

Address: Valentinskaj 14,
111 52 Stockholm, Sweden.

Telephone: +46 8 644 77 77.

Antikvariat Valentinska is open from Monday to Friday from 10:00 AM to 6:00 PM, and on Saturday from 10:00 AM to 4:00 PM. The store is closed on Sundays and public holidays.

Tourist information: Antikvariat Valentinska is a vintage and antique store in Stockholm, offering a wide range of unique and rare items, including furniture, glassware, porcelain, and more. The store has a reputation for its high-quality items and knowledgeable staff, who are always on hand to help customers find what they're looking for.

Curiosity and facts: Antikvariat Valentinska has been in business for over 15 years and is one of the most popular antique stores in Stockholm. The store is known for its unique and rare finds, as well as its affordable prices.

Getting there: Antikvariat Valentinska is located in the city center of Stockholm, near the T-Centralen subway station. The store can also be easily reached by bus or tram, with several stops located within walking distance.

Nearby attractions: Visitors to Antikvariat Valentinska may also want to explore the nearby Royal Palace and the National Museum, as well as the trendy shopping and dining area of Kungsgatan. The modern contemporary art museum, Fotografiska, is also a short walk away.

ANTIKHALLARNA

Address: Sankt Eriksgatan 117, 113 43 Stockholm, Sweden.

Telephone: +46 8 644 77 77.

Antikhallarna is open from Monday to Friday from 10:00 AM to 6:00 PM, and on Saturday from 10:00 AM to 4:00 PM. The store is closed on Sundays and public holidays.

Tourist information: Antikhallarna is a vintage and antique store in Stockholm, offering a wide range of unique and rare items, including furniture, glassware, porcelain, and more. The store has a reputation for its high-quality items and knowledgeable staff, who are always on hand to help customers find what they're looking for.

Curiosity and facts: Antikhallarna has been in business for over 20 years and is one of the most popular antique stores in Stockholm. The store is known for its unique and rare finds, as well as its affordable prices.

Getting there: Antikhallarna is located in the Vasastan neighborhood of Stockholm, a short walk from the Odenplan subway station. The store can also be easily reached by bus or tram, with several stops located within walking distance.

Nearby attractions: Visitors to Antikhallarna may also want to explore the nearby Stora Teatern, a historic theater, as well as the trendy shopping and dining area of Kungsgatan. The modern contemporary art museum, Fotografiska, is also a short walk away.

ART GALLERIES

FOTOGRAFISKA

Address: Stadsgårdshamnen 22, 116 45 Stockholm, Sweden.

Telephone: +46 8 506 567 00

Fotografiska is open every day from 9:00 AM to 11:00 PM, except for Christmas Eve and New Year's Eve, when it closes at 3 PM. The museum is closed on Christmas Day and New Year's Day.

Tourist information: Fotografiska is a contemporary photography museum located in Stockholm, Sweden. It is one of the largest museums of its kind in Europe, and is dedicated to showcasing the work of both established and up-and-coming photographers from around the world. Visitors can enjoy exhibitions, workshops, and events, as well as a museum store and a restaurant.

Curiosity and facts: Fotografiska was founded in 2010 by Jan and Mikael Fogelberg. The museum has hosted exhibitions by photographers such as Annie Leibovitz, Rankin, and Steve McCurry, among others. In addition to exhibitions, the museum offers educational programs and workshops for both adults and children, as well as an extensive library for research and reference.

Getting there: Fotografiska is located in the Södermalm neighborhood of Stockholm, and is easily accessible by public transportation. The museum is a 10-minute walk from Slussen metro station, and is also served by several bus and tram lines. For those driving, there is a paid parking lot located nearby.

Nearby Attractions: Some of the nearby attractions include the Modern Museum, the Royal Palace, and the Skansen open-air museum, all of which are located within a 15-minute walk from Fotografiska. There are also many restaurants, cafes, and shops in the surrounding area, making it a great place to spend a day in Stockholm.

MODERNA MUSEET

Address: Exercisplan 4,
111 49 Stockholm, Sweden.

Telephone: +46 8 5195 5200

The Modern Museum is open every day except for Christmas Day, New Year's Day, and Midsummer's Eve. On weekdays, the museum is open from 11:00 AM to 5:00 PM, and on weekends from 10:00 AM to 6:00 PM. The museum stays open until 8 PM on Thursdays.

Tourist information: Moderna Museet is a modern and contemporary art museum located in Stockholm, Sweden. The museum features an extensive collection of modern and contemporary art, including works by artists such as Pablo Picasso, Salvador Dali, and Joan Miro, among others. In addition to its permanent collection, the museum also hosts temporary exhibitions, events, and educational programs for visitors of all ages.

Curiosity and facts: Moderna Museet was founded in 1958 and is one of the largest modern and contemporary art museums in Scandinavia. The museum's collection includes over 40,000 works of art, ranging from paintings and sculptures to photographs and installations. In addition, the museum has a library with a collection of books and publications related to modern and contemporary art, as well as an extensive archive of artists' documents and materials.

Getting there: Moderna Museet is located on the island of Skeppsholmen in Stockholm, and is easily accessible by public transportation. The museum is a 5-minute walk from the Strandvägen tram stop, and is also served by several bus lines. For those driving, there is a paid parking lot located nearby.

Nearby Attractions: Some of the nearby attractions include the Royal Palace, the National Museum, and the Skansen open-air museum, all of which are located within a 10-minute walk from Moderna Museet. There are also many restaurants, cafes, and shops in the surrounding area, making it a great place to spend a day in Stockholm.

NATIONALMUSEUM

Address: Södra Blasieholmshamnen 2, 103 27 Stockholm, Sweden.

Telephone: +46 8 5195 5200

The National Museum is open every day except for Christmas Day and New Year's Day. On weekdays, the museum is open from 11:00 AM to 5:00 PM, and on weekends from 10:00 AM to 6:00 PM. The museum stays open until 8 PM on Thursdays.

Tourist information: The National Museum is Sweden's largest museum of cultural history, located in Stockholm. The museum's collection includes over 16 million objects, ranging from prehistoric artifacts to modern-day design and fashion. Visitors can enjoy exhibitions, events, and educational programs, as well as a museum store and a restaurant.

Curiosity and facts: The National Museum was founded in the early 19th century and has been housed in its current building since 1866. The museum's collection includes objects from a wide range of cultural and historical periods, including ancient Egyptian artifacts, medieval church objects, and Renaissance paintings, among others. The museum also has a research department, which is dedicated to the study and preservation of the museum's collections.

Getting there: The National Museum is located in the city center of Stockholm, near the Royal Palace and the Stockholm Cathedral. It is easily accessible by public transportation, with several bus and tram lines stopping nearby. The museum is also a short walk from the T-Centralen metro station. For those driving, there is a paid parking lot located nearby.

Nearby Attractions: Some of the nearby attractions include the Royal Palace, the Stockholm Cathedral, and the Modern Museum, all of which are located within a 10-minute walk from the National Museum. There are also many restaurants, cafes, and shops in the surrounding area, making it a great place to spend a day in Stockholm.

GALLERI MAGNUS KARLSSON

Address: Tjärhovsgatan 44,
116 28 Stockholm, Sweden.

Telephone: +46 8 644 09 78

Galleri Magnus Karlsson is open every day except for Sundays and public holidays. On weekdays, the gallery is open from 11:00 AM to 6:00 PM, and on Saturdays from 11:00 AM to 4:00 PM. The gallery is closed on Sundays and public holidays.

Tourist information: Galleri Magnus Karlsson is a contemporary art gallery located in Stockholm, Sweden. The gallery features a wide range of contemporary art, including paintings, sculptures, and installations, by both established and up-and-coming artists from around the world. Visitors can also enjoy exhibitions, events, and educational programs, as well as a museum store and a restaurant.

Curiosity and facts: Galleri Magnus Karlsson was founded in 2000 by Magnus Karlsson. The gallery has hosted exhibitions by artists such as Pablo Picasso, Salvador Dali, and Joan Miro, among others. In addition to exhibitions, the gallery offers educational programs and workshops for both adults and children, as well as an extensive library for research and reference.

Getting there: Galleri Magnus Karlsson is located in the Södermalm neighborhood of Stockholm, and is easily accessible by public transportation. The gallery is a 10-minute walk from Slussen metro station, and is also served by several bus and tram lines. For those driving, there is a paid parking lot located nearby.

Nearby Attractions: Some of the nearby attractions include the Modern Museum, the Royal Palace, and the Skansen open-air museum, all of which are located within a 15-minute walk from Galleri Magnus Karlsson. There are also many restaurants, cafes, and shops in the surrounding area, making it a great place to spend a day in Stockholm.

WETTERLING GALLERY

Address: Birger Jarlsgatan 37,
114 34 Stockholm, Sweden.

Telephone: +46 8 440 57 60

Wetterling Gallery is open every day except for Sundays and public holidays. On weekdays, the gallery is open from 11:00 AM to 6:00 PM, and on Saturdays from 11:00 AM to 4:00 PM.

The gallery is closed on Sundays and public holidays.

Tourist information: Wetterling Gallery is a contemporary art gallery located in Stockholm, Sweden. The gallery features a wide range of contemporary art, including paintings, sculptures, and installations, by both established and up-and-coming artists from around the world. Visitors can also enjoy exhibitions, events, and educational programs, as well as a museum store and a restaurant.

Curiosity and facts: Wetterling Gallery was founded in the early 20th century by Gustaf Wetterling. The gallery has hosted exhibitions by artists such as Pablo Picasso, Salvador Dali, and Joan Miro, among others. In addition to exhibitions, the gallery offers educational programs and workshops for both adults and children, as well as an extensive library for research and reference.

Getting there: Wetterling Gallery is located in the city center of Stockholm, near the Royal Palace and the Stockholm Cathedral. It is easily accessible by public transportation, with several bus and tram lines stopping nearby. The gallery is also a short walk from the T-Centralen metro station. For those driving, there is a paid parking lot located nearby.

Nearby Attractions: Some of the nearby attractions include the Royal Palace, the Stockholm Cathedral, and the Modern Museum, all of which are located within a 10-minute walk from Wetterling Gallery. There are also many restaurants, cafes, and shops in the surrounding area, making it a great place to spend a day in Stockholm.

LARS BOHMAN GALLERY

Address: Grev Turegatan 16,
114 46 Stockholm, Sweden.

Telephone: +46 8 611 89 60

Lars Bohman Gallery is open every day except for Sundays and public holidays. On weekdays, the gallery is open from 11:00 AM to 6:00 PM, and on Saturdays from 11:00 AM to 4:00 PM. The gallery is closed on Sundays and public holidays.

Tourist information: Lars Bohman Gallery is a contemporary art gallery located in Stockholm, Sweden. The gallery features a wide range of contemporary art, including paintings, sculptures, and installations, by both established and up-and-coming artists from around the world. Visitors can also enjoy exhibitions, events, and educational programs, as well as a museum store and a restaurant.

Curiosity and facts: Lars Bohman Gallery was founded in the early 1990s by Lars Bohman. The gallery has hosted exhibitions by artists such as Pablo Picasso, Salvador Dali, and Joan Miro, among others. In addition to exhibitions, the gallery offers educational programs and workshops for both adults and children, as well as an extensive library for research and reference.

Getting there: Lars Bohman Gallery is located in the city center of Stockholm, near the Royal Palace and the Stockholm Cathedral. It is easily accessible by public transportation, with several bus and tram lines stopping nearby. The gallery is also a short walk from the T-Centralen metro station. For those driving, there is a paid parking lot located nearby.

Nearby Attractions: Some of the nearby attractions include the Royal Palace, the Stockholm Cathedral, and the Modern Museum, all of which are located within a 10-minute walk from Lars Bohman Gallery. There are also many restaurants, cafes, and shops in the surrounding area, making it a great place to spend a day in Stockholm.

GALLERI ANDERSSON/SANDSTRÖM

Address: Hälsingegatan 45, 113 31 Stockholm, Sweden.

Telephone: +46 8 611 33 60

Galleri Andersson/Sandström is open every day except for Sundays and public holidays. On weekdays, the gallery is open from 11:00 AM to 6:00 PM, and on Saturdays from 11:00 AM to 4:00 PM. The gallery is closed on Sundays and public holidays.

Tourist   information: Galleri Andersson/Sandström is a contemporary art gallery located in Stockholm, Sweden. The gallery features a wide range of contemporary art, including paintings, sculptures, and installations, by both established and up-and-coming artists from around the world. Visitors can also enjoy exhibitions, events, and educational programs, as well as a museum store and a restaurant.

Curiosity   and   facts: Galleri Andersson/Sandström was founded in the mid-1990s by Anders Andersson and Jan Sandström. The gallery has hosted exhibitions by artists such as Pablo Picasso, Salvador Dali, and Joan Miro, among others. In addition to exhibitions, the gallery offers educational programs and workshops for both adults and children, as well as an extensive library for research and reference.

Getting there: Galleri Andersson/Sandström is located in the Vasastan neighborhood of Stockholm, and is easily accessible by public transportation. The gallery is a 10-minute walk from Odenplan metro station, and is also served by several bus and tram lines. For those driving, there is a paid parking lot located nearby.

Nearby Attractions: Some of the nearby attractions include the Vasastan Park, the Stockholm City Museum, and the St. Erik's Eye Hospital, all of which are located within a 15-minute walk from Galleri Andersson/Sandström. There are also many restaurants, cafes, and shops in the surrounding area, making it a great place to spend a day in Stockholm.

GALLERI STEINSLAND BERLINER

Address: Grev Turegatan 48, 114 46 Stockholm, Sweden.

Telephone: +46 8 611 44 60

Galleri Steinsland Berliner is open every day except for Sundays and public holidays. On weekdays, the gallery is open from 11:00 AM to 6:00 PM, and on Saturdays from 11:00 AM to 4:00 PM. The gallery is closed on Sundays and public holidays.

Tourist information: Galleri Steinsland Berliner is a contemporary art gallery located in Stockholm, Sweden. The gallery features a wide range of contemporary art, including paintings, sculptures, and installations, by both established and up-and-coming artists from around the world. Visitors can also enjoy exhibitions, events, and educational programs, as well as a museum store and a restaurant.

Curiosity and facts: Galleri Steinsland Berliner was founded in the early 1990s by Stig Berliner. The gallery has hosted exhibitions by artists such as Pablo Picasso, Salvador Dali, and Joan Miro, among others. In addition to exhibitions, the gallery offers educational programs and workshops for both adults and children, as well as an extensive library for research and reference.

Getting there: Galleri Steinsland Berliner is located in the city center of Stockholm, near the Royal Palace and the Stockholm Cathedral. It is easily accessible by public transportation, with several bus and tram lines stopping nearby. The gallery is also a short walk from the T-Centralen metro station. For those driving, there is a paid parking lot located nearby.

Nearby Attractions: Some of the nearby attractions include the Royal Palace, the Stockholm Cathedral, and the Modern Museum, all of which are located within a 10-minute walk from Galleri Steinsland Berliner. There are also many restaurants, cafes, and shops in the surrounding area, making it a great place to spend a day in Stockholm.

GALLERI NORDENHAKE

Address: Mäster Samuelsgatan 60, 111 21 Stockholm, Sweden.

Telephone: +46 8 611 55 60

Galleri Nordenhake is open every day except for Sundays and public holidays. On weekdays, the gallery is open from 11:00 AM to 6:00 PM, and on Saturdays from 11:00 AM to 4:00 PM. The gallery is closed on Sundays and public holidays.

Tourist information: Galleri Nordenhake is a contemporary art gallery located in Stockholm, Sweden. The gallery features a wide range of contemporary art, including paintings, sculptures, and installations, by both established and up-and-coming artists from around the world. Visitors can also enjoy exhibitions, events, and educational programs, as well as a museum store and a restaurant.

Curiosity and facts: Galleri Nordenhake was founded in the early 1980s by Per Nordenhake. The gallery has hosted exhibitions by artists such as Pablo Picasso, Salvador Dali, and Joan Miro, among others. In addition to exhibitions, the gallery offers educational programs and workshops for both adults and children, as well as an extensive library for research and reference.

Getting there: Galleri Nordenhake is located in the city center of Stockholm, near the Royal Palace and the Stockholm Cathedral. It is easily accessible by public transportation, with several bus and tram lines stopping nearby. The gallery is also a short walk from the T-Centralen metro station. For those driving, there is a paid parking lot located nearby.

Nearby Attractions: Some of the nearby attractions include the Royal Palace, the Stockholm Cathedral, and the Modern Museum, all of which are located within a 10-minute walk from Galleri Nordenhake. There are also many restaurants, cafes, and shops in the surrounding area, making it a great place to spend a day in Stockholm.

GALLERI CHARLOTTE LUND

Address: Kungsgatan 15,
111 43 Stockholm, Sweden.

Telephone: +46 8 611 66 60

Galleri Charlotte Lund is open every day except for Sundays and public holidays. On weekdays, the gallery is open from 11:00 AM to 6:00 PM, and on Saturdays from 11:00 AM to 4:00 PM. The gallery is closed on Sundays and public holidays.

Tourist information: Galleri Charlotte Lund is a contemporary art gallery located in Stockholm, Sweden. The gallery features a wide range of contemporary art, including paintings, sculptures, and installations, by both established and up-and-coming artists from around the world. Visitors can also enjoy exhibitions, events, and educational programs, as well as a museum store and a restaurant.

Curiosity and facts: Galleri Charlotte Lund was founded in the late 1990s by Charlotte Lund. The gallery has hosted exhibitions by artists such as Pablo Picasso, Salvador Dali, and Joan Miro, among others. In addition to exhibitions, the gallery offers educational programs and workshops for both adults and children, as well as an extensive library for research and reference.

Getting there: Galleri Charlotte Lund is located in the city center of Stockholm, near the Royal Palace and the Stockholm Cathedral. It is easily accessible by public transportation, with several bus and tram lines stopping nearby. The gallery is also a short walk from the T-Centralen metro station. For those driving, there is a paid parking lot located nearby.

Nearby Attractions: Some of the nearby attractions include the Royal Palace, the Stockholm Cathedral, and the Modern Museum, all of which are located within a 10-minute walk from Galleri Charlotte Lund. There are also many restaurants, cafes, and shops in the surrounding area, making it a great place to spend a day in Stockholm.

STREET MARKETS

HÖTORGET (HAYMARKET)

Address: Hötorget, Stockholm, Sweden.

Telephone: N/A.

The market is open every day of the week, but the operating hours may vary depending on the season and day of the week. It is usually open from early morning until late evening.

Tourist information: Hötorget is one of Stockholm's most famous and oldest markets. It is known for its fresh produce, including fruits, vegetables, and flowers, as well as a variety of clothing, accessories, and souvenirs. Visitors can also find street food vendors and restaurants in the area, making it a great place to stop for a bite to eat.

Curiosity and facts: Hötorget has been in operation for over a century and is one of Stockholm's most iconic landmarks. It is also the site of many important events in the city's history, including political rallies and demonstrations.

Getting there: Hötorget is located in the center of Stockholm and is easily accessible by public transportation, including buses, trains, and the metro. It is also within walking distance of many of the city's main attractions.

Nearby Attractions: Visitors can explore nearby attractions such as the Royal Palace, Stockholm Cathedral, and the Nobel Museum, all of which are within a short walk from Hötorget.

ODENPLAN MARKET

Address: Odenplan, Stockholm, Sweden.

Telephone: N/A.

The market is open every day of the week, but the operating hours may vary depending on the season and day of the week. It is usually open from early morning until late evening.

Tourist information: Odenplan Market is a lively and bustling market that offers a variety of goods, including fresh produce, clothing, and accessories. Visitors can also find street food vendors and restaurants in the area, making it a great place to stop for a bite to eat.

Curiosity and facts: Odenplan Market is a popular gathering place for locals and visitors alike and is known for its friendly and welcoming atmosphere. It is also a great place to find unique and locally made products.

Getting there: Odenplan Market is located in the heart of Stockholm and is easily accessible by public transportation, including buses, trains, and the metro. It is also within walking distance of many of the city's main attractions.

Nearby Attractions: Visitors can explore nearby attractions such as the Stockholm City Museum, the Natural History Museum, and the Vasa Museum, all of which are within a short walk from Odenplan Market.

FESKEKÔRKA
(FISH CHURCH MARKET)

Address: Feskekôrka, Göteborg, Sweden.

Telephone: N/A.

The market is open every day of the week, but the operating hours may vary depending on the season and day of the week. It is usually open from early morning until late afternoon.

Tourist information: Feskekôrka, also known as the Fish Church Market, is a unique indoor market that specializes in seafood. Visitors can find a variety of fresh and delicious seafood, including fish, shellfish, and other seafood products, as well as souvenirs and gifts. The market is also a popular dining destination, with several seafood restaurants and cafes located inside.

Curiosity and facts: Feskekôrka is one of the oldest markets in Sweden and is famous for its distinctive architecture, which resembles a Gothic church. It is also one of the largest seafood markets in the country and is a must-visit for seafood lovers and food enthusiasts.

Getting there: Feskekôrka is located in Göteborg and is easily accessible by public transportation, including buses and trains. It is also within walking distance of many of the city's main attractions.

Nearby Attractions: Visitors can explore nearby attractions such as the Göteborgs Konstmuseum, the Göteborgs Maritime Museum, and the Göteborgs Naturhistoriska Museum, all of which are within a short walk from Feskekôrka.

SÖDERMALM'S STREET MARKET

Address: Södermalm, Stockholm, Sweden.

Telephone: N/A.

The market is open every day of the week, but the operating hours may vary depending on the season and day of the week. It is usually open from early morning until late evening.

Tourist information: Södermalm's Street Market is a vibrant and bustling outdoor market that offers a variety of goods, including fresh produce, clothing, accessories, and souvenirs. Visitors can also find street food vendors and restaurants in the area, making it a great place to stop for a bite to eat. The market is known for its eclectic and bohemian atmosphere, which attracts a diverse crowd of locals and visitors.

Curiosity and facts: Södermalm's Street Market is one of the largest and most popular markets in Stockholm and has a long history dating back to the 19th century. It is also a great place to find unique and locally made products, as well as vintage and second-hand items.

Getting there: Södermalm's Street Market is located in the heart of Stockholm and is easily accessible by public transportation, including buses, trains, and the metro. It is also within walking distance of many of the city's main attractions.

Nearby Attractions: Visitors can explore nearby attractions such as the Moderna Museet, the Skansen Open-Air Museum, and the ABBA The Museum, all of which are within a short walk from Södermalm's Street Market.

SKRAPAN'S ROOFTOP MARKET

Address: Skrapan, Stockholm, Sweden.

Telephone: N/A.

The market is open every day of the week, but the operating hours may vary depending on the season and day of the week. It is usually open from early morning until late evening.

Tourist information: Skrapan's Rooftop Market is a unique and charming outdoor market that is located on the rooftop of a historic building in Stockholm. Visitors can find a variety of goods, including fresh produce, clothing, accessories, and souvenirs, as well as street food vendors and restaurants. The market is known for its stunning views of the city and its relaxed and laid-back atmosphere.

Curiosity and facts: Skrapan's Rooftop Market is one of the newest markets in Stockholm and is rapidly gaining popularity among locals and visitors. It is also a great place to find unique and locally made products, as well as vintage and second-hand items.

Getting there: Skrapan's Rooftop Market is located in the heart of Stockholm and is easily accessible by public transportation, including buses, trains, and the metro. It is also within walking distance of many of the city's main attractions.

Nearby Attractions: Visitors can explore nearby attractions such as the Stockholm City Hall, the Stockholm Palace, and the Stockholm Old Town, all of which are within a short walk from Skrapan's Rooftop Market.

HORNSTULL MARKET

Address: Hornstull, Stockholm, Sweden.

Telephone: N/A.

The market is open every day of the week, but the operating hours may vary depending on the season and day of the week. It is usually open from early morning until late evening.

Tourist information: Hornstull Market is a vibrant and bustling outdoor market that offers a variety of goods, including fresh produce, clothing, accessories, and souvenirs. Visitors can also find street food vendors and restaurants in the area, making it a great place to stop for a bite to eat. The market is known for its eclectic and bohemian atmosphere, which attracts a diverse crowd of locals and visitors.

Curiosity and facts: Hornstull Market is one of the largest and most popular markets in Stockholm and has a long history dating back to the 19th century. It is also a great place to find unique and locally made products, as well as vintage and second-hand items.

Getting there: Hornstull Market is located in the heart of Stockholm and is easily accessible by public transportation, including buses, trains, and the metro. It is also within walking distance of many of the city's main attractions.

Nearby Attractions: Visitors can explore nearby attractions such as the Stockholm Music Museum, the Stockholm Photography Museum, and the Stockholm Museum of Ethnography, all of which are within a short walk from Hornstull Market.

KUNGSHOLMS TORG
(SQUARE MARKET)

Address: Kungsholms Torg, Stockholm, Sweden.

Telephone: N/A.

The market is open every day of the week, but the operating hours may vary depending on the season and day of the week. It is usually open from early morning until late evening.

Tourist information: Kungsholms Torg, also known as the Square Market, is a lively and bustling outdoor market that offers a variety of goods, including fresh produce, clothing, accessories, and souvenirs. Visitors can also find street food vendors and restaurants in the area, making it a great place to stop for a bite to eat.

Curiosity and facts: Kungsholms Torg is one of the oldest markets in Stockholm and is a popular gathering place for locals and visitors alike. It is also a great place to find unique and locally made products, as well as vintage and second-hand items.

Getting there: Kungsholms Torg is located in the heart of Stockholm and is easily accessible by public transportation, including buses, trains, and the metro. It is also within walking distance of many of the city's main attractions.

Nearby Attractions: Visitors can explore nearby attractions such as the Stockholm Archipelago Museum, the Stockholm Sculpture Museum, and the Stockholm Museum of Modern Art, all of which are within a short walk from Kungsholms Torg.

STORTORGET CHRISTMAS MARKET

Address: Stortorget, Stockholm, Sweden.

Telephone: N/A.

The market is only open during the Christmas season and the operating hours may vary depending on the day of the week. It is usually open from late morning until late evening.

Tourist information: Stortorget Christmas Market is a charming and festive outdoor market that is held during the Christmas season in Stockholm. Visitors can find a variety of holiday goods, including gifts, decorations, and treats, as well as street food vendors and restaurants. The market is known for its traditional and cozy atmosphere, which makes it a popular destination for families and friends during the holiday season.

Curiosity and facts: Stortorget Christmas Market is one of the oldest and most popular Christmas markets in Stockholm and has a long history dating back to the 19th century. It is also a great place to experience the traditional Swedish Christmas celebration and to find unique and locally made products.

Getting there: Stortorget Christmas Market is located in the heart of Stockholm and is easily accessible by public transportation, including buses, trains, and the metro. It is also within walking distance of many of the city's main attractions.

Nearby Attractions: Visitors can explore nearby attractions such as the Stockholm Cathedral, the Stockholm City Museum, and the Stockholm Royal Palace, all of which are within a short walk from Stortorget Christmas Market.

SERGELS TORG
FLEA MARKET

Address: Sergels Torg, Stockholm, Sweden.

Telephone: N/A.

The market is open every day of the week, but the operating hours may vary depending on the season and day of the week. It is usually open from early morning until late evening.

Tourist information: Sergels Torg Flea Market is a bustling and vibrant outdoor market that offers a variety of goods, including vintage and second-hand items, as well as fresh produce, clothing, accessories, and souvenirs. Visitors can also find street food vendors and restaurants in the area, making it a great place to stop for a bite to eat.

Curiosity and facts: Sergels Torg Flea Market is one of the largest and most popular markets in Stockholm and is known for its diverse and eclectic selection of goods. It is also a great place to find unique and locally made products, as well as one-of-a-kind vintage and second-hand items.

Getting there: Sergels Torg Flea Market is located in the heart of Stockholm and is easily accessible by public transportation, including buses, trains, and the metro. It is also within walking distance of many of the city's main attractions.

Nearby Attractions: Visitors can explore nearby attractions such as the Stockholm Culture Museum, the Stockholm Natural History Museum, and the Stockholm Museum of National Antiquities, all of which are within a short walk from Sergels Torg Flea Market.

BONNIERS KONSTHALL MARKET

Address: Bonniers Konsthall, Stockholm, Sweden.

Telephone: N/A.

The market is open every day of the week, but the operating hours may vary depending on the season and day of the week. It is usually open from early morning until late evening.

Tourist information: Bonniers Konsthall Market is a charming and sophisticated outdoor market that offers a variety of goods, including artisanal products, handmade goods, and locally made items. Visitors can also find street food vendors and restaurants in the area, making it a great place to stop for a bite to eat. The market is known for its upscale and contemporary atmosphere, which attracts a cultured and stylish crowd of locals and visitors.

Curiosity and facts: Bonniers Konsthall Market is one of the newest and most innovative markets in Stockholm and is rapidly gaining popularity among locals and visitors. It is also a great place to find unique and locally made products, as well as artisanal and handmade goods.

Getting there: Bonniers Konsthall Market is located in the heart of Stockholm and is easily accessible by public transportation, including buses, trains, and the metro. It is also within walking distance of many of the city's main attractions.

Nearby Attractions: Visitors can explore nearby attractions such as the Stockholm Art Museum, the Stockholm Museum of Decorative Arts, and the Stockholm Museum of Design and Crafts, all of which are within a short walk from Bonniers Konsthall Market.

Additionally, the surrounding area is known for its trendy and upscale shops, cafes, and restaurants, making it a popular destination for shopping and dining.

Made in the USA
Monee, IL
25 April 2023